Terasa Gipson had worked as an academic and public librarian for over twenty years. Currently, she is an adjunct professor at SUNY Buffalo State University. Terasa lives in the Western New York area with her husband. *Rearview* is her second book.

To all the people, past and present, who continuously strive
to pivot our nation toward the betterment of everyone. Your
lives and endless efforts will never be in vain.

Terasa Gipson

REARVIEW

AUSTIN MACAULEY PUBLISHERS™
LONDON • CAMBRIDGE • NEW YORK • SHARJAH

Ordering Information
Quantity sales: Special discounts are available on quantity purchases by corporations, associations, and others. For details, contact the publisher at the address below.

Publisher's Cataloging-in-Publication data
Gipson, Terasa
Rearview

ISBN 9798889108481 (Paperback)
ISBN 9798889108498 (ePub e-book)

Library of Congress Control Number: 2023921576

www.austinmacauley.com/us

First Published 2024
Austin Macauley Publishers LLC
40 Wall Street, 33rd Floor, Suite 3302
New York, NY 10005
USA

mail-usa@austinmacauley.com
+1 (646) 5125767

To Jesus, my Lord and Savior.

To my family, friends, and all the people who have inspired and supported me. Much love, thanks, and blessings to you all.

Finally, to the people at Austin Macauley Publishers, my sincere thanks for all the work you do. I am grateful.

Tables of Contents

"Study the past if you would define the future."

– Confucius

Things Remembered

Memories

The bedrock of existence
People, places, events, and experiences
tucked away
in the hidden crevices
of the mind
preserved for an appointed time

Unexpectantly
impressions appear
surfacing as fractured images
unable to solidify

But
when the time is right
captured moments
assemble like familiar photos
flooding the senses
as unspoken words

Images of substance
fortify into concrete visions
brought back to life
before receding into
the misty shadows
until reuniting again

Retro-Flections

Thoughtful reflection
inspire new affection
for things no longer here
we once held so dear

Appreciation for the old
clings to us like pure gold

I clearly remember when
these things existed back then

The Rotary Telephone

A great invention
one person on another extension
Instrument of communication
Transmitter of information

Unique in its shapely design
operated by wires that intertwined
so people could speak on a party line
where privacy was not kept in mind

Telephone numbers then
used three-letter prefixes to begin
Five to seven numbers at the end
The dialer had letters and numbers to spin
This connection was a thirty-year trend

Telephone Booths

A glassed enclosure outside
that housed a telephone inside

Kept users from outdoor conditions
People used the phones in standing positions

Phone booths offered some privacy besides
Not just a changing closet for Superman to hide

Devices

Turntables, a revolving wheel to play
albums and records of the day

Tape players designed for 8-track tapes and cassettes
were the newest thing that came next

Other devices have come and gone
Cellphones are the latest swan song
until something better comes along

Typewriters

Manual or electric
compared to computers seems eccentric

If a mistake was made when typed
one grabbed the white-out to swipe

To make a copy of a sheet
had to use carbon paper to repeat

More Retro-Flections

Watched television in a big wooden box
It was called a console that squawked

American Bandstand with Dick Clark
brought in the New Year after dark

Dancing to the music from the latest grooves
like the twist and mashed potatoes were some of the moves

Locomotion, the Jerk and Boogaloo
Not to forget, the Watusi was popular too

Sunday evenings, everyone watched the Ed Sullivan Show
He introduced new talent each week to know

Banana bike seats built for two
transportation to and from school

Troll dolls, a strange novelty
crazy hair, a sight to see

Etch-a-Sketch made funny shapes
Shake really hard, and your drawing escapes

Jell-O salad molds not a current trend
Perfect for potlucks, but then again

Shake-n-Bake for family dinner
Quick, easy meal, always a winner

Tang, a sweet orange tangy drink
just add water and expect to pucker and blink

Barbie doll is still a trend
She had a male friend named Ken

She drove a pink convertible Corvette
and brought along Taffy, her pet

Milk was in glass containers delivered by a milkman
dressed in a white uniform and drove a white van

The milk was placed in a milk box
on the side of each house unlocked

These were some things once remembered
that were put aside or quietly surrendered

But
if one lives long enough to see
things repurposed into another reality
What was old is now new again
Not gone, but different from back when

Living in Community

Dividing Lines

27

Cities divided
invisible walls not built
but seen everywhere

Neighborhoods by race
lived within the same borders
relegated there

The Exodus

In the late fifties
my parents moved
into one of the city's
historic districts
known as Hamlin Park

At the time
the residents who lived there
were the first generation
immigrants of
German and Jewish decent

This hamlet community
situated in the bosom
of the city
was considered
a prime residential area

Its curbside appeal
showcased an assortment
of lush, thick trees
well-manicured lawns
two-story family homes
front porches
and fenced-in backyards

which made Hamlin Park
an attractive neighborhood
to raise a family
and reflected one's station
in life

Soon
middle-class
African Americans
with financial standing
captivated by Hamlet's charm
purchased homes
in the district

As more African Americans
moved into the neighborhood
the previous residents
moved out
Their arrival
was not the image
of community
originally perceived or
sought after

In time
the landscape shifted
with its new residents
devoted to preserving
the high standards
of Hamlin Park
for future generations

Growing up in this
section of the city
no matter its transition
there was never a question
of who I was
or where I belonged

I was home

Our Neighborhood

Summertime
in the neighborhood
was absorbed
in vibrant activity

Everywhere
life was in constant motion

Our house
sat on the corner
surrounded by
a cornucopia of sights
and sounds

Children played games
in the street
Their laughter heard for miles

Chalk drawings on asphalt
and hopscotched sidewalks
portrayed artful passions
in quiet playtime
Thick clouds of savory smoke
blanketed the neighborhood
with the aroma

of barbeque chicken and ribs
smeared with homemade sauce
grilled to perfection
ready for purchase

The corner store
a penny candy haven
enticed wide-eyed youngsters
with big wants
and tiny budgets
asking the store clerk
what can be bought
with a few cents

After dinner
neighbors gathered
on their porches
a front-row seat
to the panoramic scene
of travelers through the streets

Friendly passersby
wave a hand

Gentlemen tipped their hat
or gave a nod
as polite greetings of acknowledgement

Families out
for an evening stroll
shared sidewalks

with couples
who held hands
Their silent language
seen by all who understood

Vietnam Veterans
home from the war
injured and dejected
navigated through
the neighborhood
deflected bewildered stares
from curious onlookers
as they adjusted
to their new normal

At dusk
teenage boys
dubbed "The Street Corner Symphony"
stood under the halo
of the streetlights
to perform
a musical concert
sung a cappella style

Their harmonious voices
bellowed into the night
melodies of love, peace
heartbreak and hope
Their gift enchanted listeners
like a soothing balm
as a bedtime lullaby

for a longing
not yet satisfied

Our community
rich in connection
steeped in cultural wealth
gave way to a sense
of togetherness and acceptance
unmatched by life
outside its perimeter

Strange Canvas

On the first day of school
high school freshmen
sprinted through the neighborhood
after dismissal
headed home

Their heads bowed low

As they passed by
I saw littered faces
of lipstick, shoe polish
chalk and crayons
used like paintbrushes
across a moving canvas

Clothes disheveled
some torn
from hands that clawed
at its accosted targets
attempting to expose
more skin for markings
like billboards
for unwelcomed advertisement

Students soaked in
embarrassment and shame
made to resemble
a scribbled page
from a children's coloring book

Jagged patterns of graffiti
scrawled across their bodies
as if boundary lines
did not exist

Bystanders watched
unconcerned
while older teens
gathered around those
who could not escape
the intrusion

Most endured
freshman initiation

It was understood
as something that must take place
as it had generations before

It was a rite of passage

For decades now
this custom
is no longer
an accepted practice

to perform on incoming
high schoolers

Although abolished
past recipients
can still see
in the mirror of their minds
the invisible markings
obscured from view
but deeply remembered

Bypass for Progress

Every day
I used to walk to elementary school
along tree-lined streets
and well-preserved homes
in the Hamlin Park district
where I lived

Even as a child
I took notice of the
neighborhood's beauty

Planted down the middle
of the street
in front of my school
was a grassy island
filled with huge trees
rooted deep in their soil
which spanned the island
from one end to the other

a testament to their longevity
as the first residents
in the community

Such a vision of
magnificent elegance
that the birds paused
from their flight activity
to perch on their limbs

The island park
an Olmstead creation
used for recreation and leisure
was one of historic significance

an attractive landmark
within the inner city

One morning
on the way to school
the sound of buzz saws
and the sight of dump trucks
halted my steps

The air was sucked
from my lungs

Hundreds of trees
stood as stumps
above the ground

The majestic landmark
had been demolished
to make way
for an expressway

that would split the
African American neighborhood
as an answer to traffic flow
in and out of the city

Trees, grass, and flowers
replaced with asphalt roads
and towering cement walls
designed to camouflage
the activity below

It stripped a community
of its century-old
symbol of beauty
to become an unwanted
fortress of divide

A stark revelation of injustice
to those who had no power
to avert the decision

The impact of that verdict
is still seen and felt today

Those who lived
among the precious landscape
witnessed the destruction
which brought much sorrow
and heartbreak

Now
lost to those
who bypass the neighborhood
on their way
to somewhere else
not realizing
or ever knew
the cost others had to bear
for progress

Sunday Morning Worship

Early on Sunday
folks rose to worship the Lord
but not as one race

Places of worship
separated by color
though we served one God

He made us all
like a colorful display
Who are we to judge

Church Service at C. O. G. I.C.

(Church of God in Christ)

Each week, Sunday school
to learn from God's word, His tool
The Ten Commandments, His rules
to those who believe

In the sanctuary, further teaching
from the pastor doing the preaching
He hopes his words are reaching
hearts and souls to receive

Praise and worship to begin
Sunday service with a hymn
songs that stir from within
silent prayers lifted up

At the close of service, all rise to their feet
take the time to meet and greet
Welcome newcomers and offer a treat
togetherness in the church to build up

The Saints

When older
attended another church across town
Inside, the mood was solemn all around
Lit candles brought much light
Prayers for loved ones and worldly blight

Took notice of the various races
Filled the pew and altar spaces
unlike what I have seen before
Surprised by this revelation and more

Women wore a head covering made of lace
to cover their crown, but not their face
A sign of humility before the Lord
as something that is cherished and adored

Words spoken in Latin by the priest
Meditations read aloud when ceased
A homily to follow as explanation
Given to parishioners for spiritual edification

Kneel, stand in worship and prayer
Words rise from souls that bear
the hardened knees from years to bend
for the one who did ascend

Made right the unrighteous by grace
and stood willingly in our place
to suffer the wrath of God on the cross
so, we could be saved from death and loss

Broken Barriers

Raw Territory

By the time
I moved up to seventh grade
schools in our city
bussed students
from neighborhood schools
in the black communities
to schools outside their area

Boundary lines
of racial separation
slowly pushed
its way through
the spaces of divide

Many
did not embrace
the new way

It was not
how things should be
they'd say

Black children
White children
attending the same schools

seated in the same classrooms
next to each other
learning under one teacher
a nuance
unlike before
some whites moved
to the suburbs
where schools
and neighborhoods
seemed untouched
by the new direction
thought to be a quick solution
to a much deeper problem
Black parents
apprehensive for their children
traveling to unfamiliar environments
far away from home
unsure of how their presence
would be received

They had to decide
if the long-term benefits
outweighed
the present circumstances
Numerous black educators
experienced layoffs
or job loss

with the transfer of their students
to other schools

People clothed in defiance
against the gravitational pull
of an uncertain vision
could not see the value
of such a merger

Resistance prompted
acts of rebellion
believed that if
enough white children
were kept out of school
or transferred to private education
laws would revert back
to what they had been

People could resume
their accepted way of life

Bomb threats
Death threats
Protests
could not alter the day

Angry crowds
acting as barricades
to stop the tidal wave of change
pounding against the rocky shores
of the nation
could not prevent
what was meant to be

Another force was at work
stronger than the wanton acts
of the masses

In the twilight of transformation
emerged a different reality

The new arrival
of multicolored complexions
textured hair
unique ways of expression
made it clear
that the movement
had seeped into the fabric
of their communities

Students had a host
of mixed reactions
to these newcomers
who had infiltrated their orbit

Many students made efforts
to extend an olive branch
disregarding social norms

Neighbors surrounding schools
that did not have a cafeteria
opened up their homes
to host black students during lunchtime
In doing so
unknowingly filled

a crack in the divide

Still other students
whose perceptions
mimicked the notions
of significant adults
were too inexperienced
to possess the depth
of understanding on their own

Yet
many sought
to cradle the transformation
with a sincere willingness
in the hope of carving
a better future

The chance
to live, be educated, and work
in community
with mutual respect
and acceptance

Pooling together
resources, skills, and talents
to create a stronger nation
with relentless endurance
and resolve

An Educational Nightmare

Sixth grade
a difficult time
for a twelve-year-old

Many changes
taking place
in the mind and body

Evidence of it
shows up
bearing witness
to one's becoming

The year I became a sixth grader
sex education became
an approved course
to teach in public school

Permission slips
were passed out
to be signed by parents and returned

Each week
students were summoned
to the auditorium

to watch a film
projected on a large screen
about the body's transition
from childhood to adulthood

Descriptions of how the body changes
the chemical reaction
that takes place
between a man and a woman
the act of fourplay
as a sexual prelude

The physical engagement
between a couple
which could lead to pregnancy
as a result
produced as much fear
as it did curiosity
Snickers, whispers, and laughter
circulated the auditorium

Teachers quieted their students
to no avail

The enlightenment
competed with immaturity

Students were not ready
to listen to such teaching
but curious to try it out
The awareness

brought on a barrage
of taunts
unwanted feel-ups
hand swipes across the rear
while passing in the school halls

Every day
girls were chased home
by the boys in class
hoping to take something
that did not belong to them
nor that they fully understood

Survival meant
getting ahead of the chase

As soon as the dismissal bell rang
my friends and I stood at the door
ready to blast them
and run like track stars
all the way home

Eventually
the boys grew weary
of the chase
without the gain of any rewards
and decided to go after
other girls
who soon learned
how to run like the wind

A Generational Truth

Daughters refused
the right to higher education

Believed the investment
would be wasted
when marriage and children
take precedence over careers

Young girls
guided toward
directions considered
acceptable standards
for adult women

By adolescence
struggles emerge
between internal passions
and external expectations
keeping balance
on the far side
of achievement

Generational beliefs
passed down
through time

are chains that
shackle the spirit

Women
were created
the same as men
to live side by side
equal in all things
with life and purpose
together

Threads That Bind

The Five Senses of Music

1.) Feeling

Music burrows deep
into the marrow
pulsating the inner workings
of the soul

2.) Flavor

Infused utterances of experience
flow from the
core of life

3.) Smell

Like the scent of a lover
bathed in sensuality

Anticipation of arousal
awaiting fulfillment

4.) Taste

Absorbed by its
rich sweet expression

erected from the reality
hidden underneath

5.) Language

Vibrations
communicating a message
plainly understood

An Evening at the Jazz Club

Fancy cars
decorated neighborhood streets
surrounding the colored nightclub

People arrived
ragged out in their finest attire

Swaddled in long fur coats
decorated with sparkled jewelry
fashioned in the latest hairstyles

A display of dazzle and attitude

Inside the club
tinted windows
shaded the inner space

Smokey colors
lathered the walls
accessorized with paintings
of past musicians
who jazzed their audiences
Close-set tables
enhanced the chance
for intimate connection

An atmosphere of belonging
A place of their own

Culinary delights
placed on trays
held by young servers
swirled overhead
Aromas trailed behind them

Appetites indulged
Passionate exchanges
fluttered about
the lively ambience

Patrons geared up
for they knew
it would be an evening
well spent

Musicians tuned their instruments
Heightened anticipation
garnered from onlookers

Silence drifted
throughout the room

Sultry sounds
sliced the air

Rapt attention
stilled in a moment

Heads bobbed
Toes tapped
Moods lifted
Musical notes clung
to the walls of their souls

Eclectic melodies
captivated

Spontaneous creations
mesmerized

When the music ended
everyone mingled about

Musicians praised
for their performances

Photographs taken
offered proof of bragging rights
to those who missed out
on the experience

A night of musical ecstasy
savored

Disco Days in the Upper Room

"Where folks went up to get down."

Red flocked print
covered the walls
Streaks of silver tint
matched the mirrored ball

Crowds aligned
outside the door
Dressed to the nines
Ready for more

Upstairs was where
everyone wanted to be
They ascend the stairs
to let go and be free

The cost of admission
no problem at all
Worth the permission
for having a ball

Drinks were served
to liven the mood
softens the nerves
for people to groove

Neon strobe lights
wooden dance floor
boogie all night
from ten to four

Folks all dressed in
bell bottoms and jumpsuits
sparkling sequins
and fancy thigh boots

Very short minis
high platform shoes
pretty much any
option you choose

Big high hair
thick sideburns
personal unique flare
everywhere you turned

Dancing to the tunes
of the disco beats
as the music looms
noise filled the streets

Doing the hustle
then the bus stop
Had to bustle
to do the robot

Doing the funky chicken
gets pushed aside
while the crowd thickens
to do the electric slide

By early morning's end
everyone is partied out
time to go home and mend
to go back, no doubt

Disco Diva

She glistened
with glitter, sparkles, and sweat
dancing through the night
without a worry or regret

By day
she traveled the world
Dashing hither and yon
captivated by the sights
of unknown places beyond

By night
she dazzled
in the beauty of soul and spirit
as a radiant rainbow
celebrating every minute

Disco Stud

He stood against the wall
eyes darting around the dance hall

Ready to showcase his coolness
with the ladies who could care less

He chose one who offered a smile
or maybe intrigued by his personal style

They twirled and swirled the dance floor
as if they had danced together before

When the music stopped playing
both returned to where they stood, awaiting

for someone else to come along
and dance with them all night long

An Ode to a Trailblazer

Man with a vision
dreamed of his own enterprise
to make a living

Turned auto garage
into a nice roller rink
for the neighborhood

The roller rink was
black-owned and operated
from many decades

Provided a place
where everyone could belong
A feeling of home

Many children came
every weekend for skating
Made friends and had fun

Learned fancy skate moves
Dancing to the music grooves
Magic roller wheels

Kids birthday parties
teen all-night skate with strobe lights
made the night special

In-between skate hours
the owner would put on skates
and rolled like a pro

Sunday night Bingo
brought in large crowds of people
hoping for a win

Now, gone are the days
since the rink has been active
Memories remain

A Redefinement

The Battle

Conflicts are fought
on many fronts

Some battles are
fought far away

Others are fought
at home

Many are fought
within

Each generation
experiences cycles of calm
followed by cyclones of disruption

Dispersed pieces of humanity
thrown into disarray
without the ability to prevent
the approaching disaster
even when there is an awareness
one is coming
In battle
there are always causalities
including those

who were not part of the fight

Scars
seen or unseen
show evidence
that a struggle
took place

Remnants of it
surface in unexpected ways

Before long,
someone pushes forward
whose anguished soul
has had ENOUGH
bravely takes the reins
to lead the way
along the battered path

Their courage calms
the turmoil among the masses

It releases others
to come alongside
to assist with the transition
doing what is necessary
to reconstruct a new course

of action
Turning losses into gain

A Reckoning

I was eleven years old
when a riot took place
in our city
the summer of 1967

While walking to
the local black-owned cleaners
to drop off clothes for my mother
I witnessed in horror
people running wild
through the streets
wielding baseball bats
plywood, bricks, and rocks
smashing storefront windows

Broken glass
crunched under my feet
I ran to the cleaners
and quickly ducked inside

The employees, along with
others who came into the cleaners
to escape the streets
watched from the window
as stores were being looted

cars pushed over on their sides
Molotov cocktails
thrown through businesses
and car windows

Chaos and confusion
ruled the moment

Black business owners
forced to place signs
in their windows
made of cardboard, paper, or paint
that read: Soul Brother or Soul Sister
to ward off the fury
of an unhinged crowd
weary of mistreatment and neglect

White store owners
fled or hid in their businesses
until the police arrived

Later
I would find out
race riots ravished city streets
across the nation
Cities shutdown
Colleges disrupted
Students staged sit-ins
Boycotts executed
Discrimination of every kind
on every level

in every area of life
levitated in disarray

A force to be reckoned with
that could no longer be ignored
or contained

It was time
for a different interpretation
of the future

One that would accept
the reality
that all its citizens
have the right to be free
with the ability to contribute
and be partakers in this
ever-evolving nation
no matter its discontent

Radical Rebels

The Black Panthers
warriors in action

They rose from the strain
of racial oppression

Fluid with ideals
to transform the masses
for what they believed
would be for the betterment
of the people

During my coming of age
I recall being intrigued
by their bold messages

Impressed with the Panthers
tenacious grip to relieve
minorities from oppressive
societal conditions and perspectives

Serious in their convictions
they set out
to address many problems
that plagued the black community

The Panthers created several
viable program incentives
with the prospect to produce
much more

Their credence for a different society
one that gave full citizenship rights
to black people on every level

The Panthers message resonated
with many young black people
and became another voice
among the many movements
which rose up in defiance
against our country's restraints
in the late sixties

However
as time passed
the Panther's became
increasingly radical
and divisive

Their good intentions
were fragmented and obscured
by less worthy activities
illegitimate to their goals

Also
other agitators and detractors
against the Black Panther's

and their mission
sought to dismantle the Party

Conflicts, opposition
and other forces
muddied the landscape
of their ambitions

A continual balancing act
to remain true to their cause
mirrored a walk
along the dotted lines
on a highway to purpose
but unable to connect
with its reality

Tainted with unsavory dealings
which proved counter-productive
to their cause
spawned the party's collapse

Pieces from the rubble
of what could-have-been
scatter across generations
like pollen in spring
seeking other visionary leaders
to re-imagine a society

who embraces its people
with respect and dignity

who chases after the truth
captures it
and turns it into positive action

who shuts the door on hate
with no space to enter

who is overwhelmed by love
compassion and kindness
without agenda

ongoing and always

Unstoppable Current

Baby Boomers
Born after WWII

Blossomed flower children
Black Power Brothers and Sisters
Civil Rights marchers
Bra burnings protestors
Women's Rights demonstrators

Emboldened
Coming of Age
Hitting the streets
changing the topography
of complacent tradition

A daring
in-your-face
attitude of expression

Welding free-style thinking
and free speech
as a way of life
Spirited declarations
of unorthodox flamboyance

Fashions
with innovative brash
bold colors and design

Sporting
long hair
large afros
dreadlocks
tied-dyed styles
beads, bandanas, and peace signs

Their unconventional ways
infused an inheritance
of alternatives
that have become possessions
in our existence today

Every sinew of life
influenced by its current

Transforming what used to be
into a cloud of dust

Our Way Our Say

Why did God make
hair like mine
Coarse, woolly, wavy, and fine

With each day
comes another test to bear
Finding new ways
to care for our hair

A search for the right products
to help with this task
makes spending small fortunes
on hair aids amassed

As women of color
we share our insights
on haircare and styles
that fancy our delights

Some straighten, some curl
others perm or weave
Whatever the style
we want to achieve

Afros, braids, locks, or twists
among the many options
that already exist

Long hair, short hair
and medium length
Even when bald
show character and strength

Our hairstyles may vary
in style and technique
which marks our beauty
as creatively unique

Worn very proudly
to work and play
whether subtle or loudly
only we have the say

So, back to the question
of why hair like mine

It's because we were made
with hands so Divine

Spiritual Revolution

The 1960's fade
in comes a new decade

Upon its arrival
came spiritual revival

On the streets
the Word was preached

TV Evangelist spreading "The Good News"
to answer those who choose

Believers handing out gospel tracts
to passersby outlining gospel facts

It was a truth to be heard
about God's Word

A new day
for a new way

Bible read
Spirit-fed

Life-giving
New living

Grace received
Hearts relieved

Truth revealed
Lost souls healed

Eyes seeing
Ears hearing

Words believed
Hope conceived

Sins confessed
Love expressed

Old ways relented
New ways presented

Salvation free
Forgiveness key

Spiritual freedom
Eternal Kingdom

Running Their Race

Visionaries

Difficult to capture
the images that run through
the corridors of their minds
waiting to be birthed

They see what no one
else sees

Each step toward their vision
sinks deeper
into the unknown
density around them

Any attempt to stand still
or turn back
slides through their grip
like sand in a tilted hourglass

Their perception
of what could be
but not yet present
is too powerful
to be suppressed

Much like a torrential force
thrusting them forward
into the light of it

So
bravely
they take hold
of possibility
and escort the way
to reality

Unfinished Business

Seated in my second-grade classroom
eyes fixed on the blackboard assignment

when abruptly
the scratchy sound
of the intercom
interrupted the quiet classroom

The school principal announced
that our President had been shot

The class sat in silence
unsure what to do

Too young to understand
the gravity of that announcement

All eyes shifted
toward the teacher
who appeared rattled
by the news

School was dismissed
Students scurried home
confused and bewildered

I arrived home
to find our living room
filled with family, friends
and neighbors
gathered around
the television
to watch the events unfold

A thick wall of people
lined the streets of Dallas
Police escorts surrounded
the motorcade containing
the President

In an instant
smiles, waves, and cheers
melted into chaos

The gathering in our home
was somber

Tears streamed down faces
Contorted expressions
registered disbelief

Some turned away
from the television screen
cutting off what could not be absorbed
in the moment

The world watched
as the President's life
disintegrated in full view

His lifeless body
laid down for the promise
of a new vision
for our country

Even as a child
I sensed darkness
had come that day

Much later
I would learn
this young President
carried the burden
of a troubled nation

His belief
was America
had the capacity
to be greater

It was a challenge
not ready to be
accepted or embraced

Unchanged minds
blinded by the roots
of racism, discrimination,

injustice, disease, and poverty
said to be
the real adversaries
in the land

Visionless to see
beyond the urgency
of the day

Barriers which weaken
rather than build-up
toward greatness

Instead
discord raged on

Made it difficult
to discern the way out

John F. Kennedy
a man who had hoped
to be a transmitter of change
never had the chance
to complete his mission
Extinguished at the battlefront

His departure
left a nation bereaved
awaiting the next
fearless leader
yet to come

A Heavy Weight

Not old enough
to see the signs
which separated
the races

Written evidence
was not posted
where my eyes could
bear witness
to the differences

Life among one's own
did not conjure up
thoughts that would lead
to questions
that could not
be answered

Not aware
of the world outside
my community

An innocent child
not yet exposed
to the contradictory ways

of society

Later
the unwritten signs
manifested in fluid motion
like fibrous tissue
feeding on its host

Bound by a structure
of generational dysfunction
of a system that
should never have been

Its powerful grasp
choking out the very breath
it needs for its own nourishment
to survive

What will it take
to draw new breath

How things were
cannot continue
to inhabit the domain

Just moving forward
is not the way

Any form of deflective shifting
will not be sustainable

It will not solve
what matters most

A collision of distinctions
diminishes the power
of what was meant to exist
in all variety and manner
bereft of explanation
excuse, apology, or cost

The right to life, liberty
and the pursuit of happiness
is for
every
living
soul

High Stakes

Dust-like mist
coats the air
People marching
from everywhere

Walking for a purpose
headed toward change
Focused determination
controlled their exchange

People of color
time to take note
The law has passed
Get ready to vote

Those not pleased
challenged the law
Provoked civil unease
to invoke those to withdrawal

A country divided
will not stand
We must be united
every woman, every man

When everyone contributes
the nation benefits
Its strength resolute
Its power unlimited

Our legacy's past
of injustice and bigotry
must not cling steadfast
to future responsibility

To vote is a right
one must not deny
It's not a casual invite
The stakes are too high

Overcast

Eyes locked forward
Ears attuned
as a black man
stood before the nation
speaking words of hope
from a dream he had

On that day
spirits were lifted
exuberance for renewal
was at hand

The vision of that dream
presented before the crowd
wrapped around
each one of them

People longing
for the country
to be transformed

Many years
have passed
since that miraculous day

Dr. Martin Luther King Jr's
foresight
of a time yet to come
has arrived in fractured pieces
as a complexed puzzle
still being assembled together

A waltz practiced
time and again
without ever getting it right

Surely
the dream spoken
to the masses
did not rest
upon one man
to accomplish

Nor did it only
fall on the ears

who heard it
at that time

His dream
was a call to action
for every generation
then and now

We see particles of it
in the workplace
in our families
in churches and society

but not with the full
tenacity of response

The vision
seeps through
a dim ray of light
always slightly above
the horizon
not ready to manifest
its brilliance

Nonetheless
even in the dark
beams of hope
illuminate the night
accompanied by the chance
of a new beginning
every day

Courage of Steel

The sixties and seventies
a time of upheavals
rising from the cinders
of past and present conditions

During this turbulent time
I was in high school

I remember being fascinated
with these new voices
speaking out against
the establishment

Absorbed by these
fighters for change and justice
I read, heard speeches
watched protests on the news
yearning to know more

Their words and bravery
were inspiration
to my youthful, rebellious soul

Then
a woman warrior
emerged out of the dissension
to become an empress of justice
for those whose muffled voices
could not break through
the surface
of the powerful

Endowed with the skills
of an educated ambassador
she fought to secure
the rights of people
crushed by societal iniquities

The first black woman
to be seated in Congress
forged a road
to a higher cause
breaking convention
changing the dynamics
of the Old Guard
to make room
for another seat at the table

A run for the presidency

Despite the odds
of such a seat
her brazen assurance
refused to accept
the status quo of the day

Her impact parted the way
for other women
and people of color

fusing forces
to erect a nation
with new variety
and vitality

Her name

Shirley Anita St. Hill Chisholm:

A woman with the courage of steel

A mighty warrior

Lest We Forget

Rearview

The past is a great teacher
for the future

Every generation
becomes aware of a former time

Previous lives and circumstances
offer clues to inform those
who follow

What we leave behind
will be for others to glean

For our lives now
are the future's past

Uprooted

A people
skin bathed
in the sun-soaked radiance
of the Motherland

Taken from their native country
Ripped from those they knew
and all that was familiar

Suffered the turbulent waters
of the sea

Endured the cruelty
of their passage

Bore the heaviness
of their circumstance

Thick with wariness and fear
that burned like the midday sun

Their feet set on strange soil
Foreign in sight and speech

They were bought and sold
Families pulled apart

Chained to the aspirations
of their possessors
to produce the fruit of wealth
and prosperity

Bodies of iron strength
Wages of sweat and blood

The cost of their birth
was the place of their grief

A people who
faced unthinkable difficulties
throughout their days and nights
were never to receive
full citizenship
in the nation
they helped
to immensely enrich

Generational survivors
of Civil War
Jim Crow, Civil Rights

racism, place-ism
which continues to chew away
at the connective joints
of our nation

By God's grace
pressed forward
with fortified courage
to produce a new crop

A distinctly different people
who changed the original intent
of enslavement to citizenship

Bearers of a complex heritage
forever making remarkable strides
together

The Celebration

Listen to the heartbeat
of the drums
Feet clapping to its vibrations

Voices lifted up
through the clouds in song

Hands stretched outward
in unity

Bodies contorted in elation
Eyes dancing upward
praising God

Can you hear the sound of freedom
Can you see its expression

Do you feel the heavy garb of oppression
fall to the ground
trampled underfoot

Far away
across the ocean and sea
cries of deliverance
rumble through the villages

into the bush of Africa
relieved for the liberation
of its own

A day to celebrate
the freeing of enslaved black people

A day to recognize
lives worthy of honor and respect

A day of coming together
to enjoy shared interest and enjoyment
of music, dance, art, and food

A day to always remember
to press on like champions
for the betterment of all people
Lest we forget

A New Trade

When racial hatred rears its might
it provokes indignation from within
Men and women rise up to fight
Exhausted by the way things have been

No longer able to bear
inflictions which scar the soul
much too long to err
for wounds to be made whole

Those condemned committed no sin
deserving of this charge
Judged by the color of their skin
the penalty unthinkably large

The cost of hatred is very high
The debt could never be paid
Unless there is an abundant supply
of love and acceptance to trade